# WORSHIP THE KING

**Hymn Arrangements for Piano and Organ
by Ron and Linda Sprunger**

*Organ*—Moderate     *Piano*—Moderately Advanced

## CONTENTS

| | |
|---|---|
| **ARIOSO** | 40 |
| *optional instrumental solo part* | 67 |
| **NEAR THE CROSS OF JESUS** | 55 |
| Near the Cross | 55 |
| Beneath the Cross of Jesus | 61 |
| **O HOLY NIGHT** | 45 |
| **THE SOLID ROCK** | 5 |
| **WORSHIP SUITE** | 14 |
| O Worship the King | 14 |
| Brethren, We Have Met to Worship | 18 |
| Breathe on Me, Breath of God | 21 |
| Set My Spirit Free | 24 |
| Holy God, We Praise Thy Name | 27 |
| I Adore You | 31 |
| *vocal leadsheet* | 66 |
| Fairest Lord Jesus | 37 |

Copyright © 1993 by Lillenas Publishing Co.
All rights reserved. Litho in U.S.A.

**Lillenas PUBLISHING COMPANY**
KANSAS CITY, MO 64141

# ABOUT THE ARRANGEMENTS

**The Solid Rock** is a hymn that reminds us that our faith, hope, and trust should be in Christ, and Christ alone, regardless of life's circumstances. In this arrangement the change of mood in stanza two is underscored by a change to the minor mode. To express the words of stanza three, the tune known as MELITA is used. (If your congregation has never sung this marriage of text and tune before, suggest they try it. It's an exhilarating change of pace!) For the final stanza, which speaks of Christ's triumphant return, the tune SOLID ROCK reenters. *Note: the congregation may be invited to stand and sing the final stanza in unison.*

**Worship Suite** is a collection of hymns and choruses that:
1. invite us to worship ("O Worship the King");
2. express the corporate nature of our worship and our need for the enabling power of the Holy Spirit ("Brethren, We Have Met to Worship"; "Breath on Me, Breath of God"; "Set My Spirit Free");
3. draw our attention to the One who alone is worthy of our praise and adoration ("Holy God, We Praise Thy Name"; "I Adore You"; and "Fairest Lord Jesus").

An optional final cadence (song ending) is included at the end of each song to facilitate the use of shorter segments of the suite for specific purposes:
   A. Thematic preludes
      1. Praise and adoration (meas. 98-184)
      2. Invocation of the Holy Spirit (meas. 57-97)
   B. Free harmonizations for the unison singing of the final stanza of the hymn
      1. "Holy God, We Praise Thy Name" (meas. 106-129)
      2. "Fairest Lord Jesus" (meas. 187-201, beat 1)
   C. Extended introductions for hymns
      1. "O Worship the King" (meas. 1-16)
      2. "Brethren, We Have Met to Worship" (meas. 39-55)
      3. "Holy God, We Praise Thy Name" (meas. 106-129)
   D. Invocations
      The congregation (assisted by the choir) could sing when the musicians come to "Breath on Me, Breath of God," "Set My Spirit Free," or "I Adore You." *Note: the leadsheet for "I Adore You" is included on p. 66, so that the congregation may learn it ahead of time. It may be duplicated under the terms of your CCLI license.*

**Arioso** by J. S. Bach is a lovely melody that conveys a beautiful sense of God's peace that is ours as we rest in Him. This piece is very appropriate for various parts of the wedding ceremony—prelude, candlelighting, bridesmaids' processional, etc. *Note: the melody from the organ score may be assigned to a solo instrument, in which case the organist would play the left hand and pedal line as soft support, along with the piano counterpart. A solo part for C instrument is included on p. 67.*

***O Holy Night*** is a Christmas favorite that recalls the wonders of that first Christmas night. Like the shepherds and wise men of old, our response should be to "fall on our knees" in humble adoration. There is "a thrill of hope" as we hear the glorious gospel message again.

***Near the Cross of Jesus*** is a medley of two hymns, "Near the Cross" and "Beneath the Cross of Jesus," reminding us that our sins are forgiven only because of the blood of Jesus Christ, given as full atonement. The phrase, "In the cross, in the cross be my glory ever," refers to Galatians 6:14, "God forbid that I should glory, save in the cross of our Lord . . ." To kneel at the foot of the Cross gives us a correct perspective from which to view "the wonders of redeeming love." *Note: for this and other selections, the hymn numbers may be included in the bulletin, along with the titles, as an encouragement to the worshiper to reflect on the words while listening.*

THE SPRUNGERS

# The Solid Rock

Sw. Solo trumpet 8'
Gt. Prin. 8',4', 2'
Ped. 16', 8'

"Solid Rock" WILLIAM. B. BRADBURY
"Melita" JOHN B. DYKES
*Arr. by Ron and Linda Sprunger*

EDWARD MOTE

Arr. © 1993 by Lillenas Publishing Co. All rights reserved.
Administered by Integrated Copyright Group, Inc., P.O. Box 24149, Nashville, TN 37202.

soul gives way, He then is all my hope and stay. On

Christ, the sol-id Rock, I stand; All oth-er ground is sink-ing

12

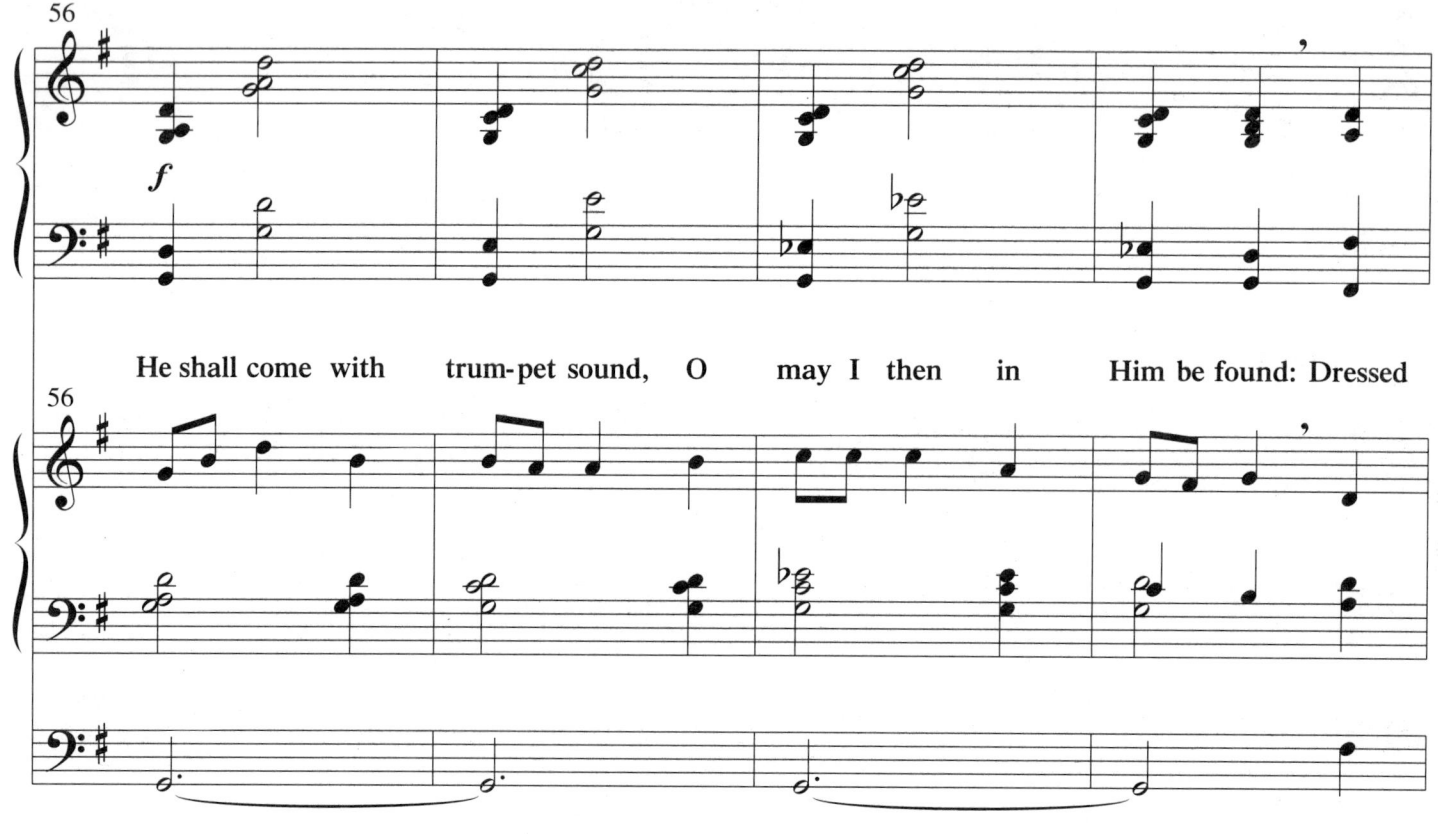

# Worship Suite

Sw. Solo reed
Gt. Soft diap. 8', 4'
Ped. 16', 8', 4'

*Arr. by Ron and Linda Sprunger*

*"O Worship the King" (Grant - Johann M. Haydn)

*Arr. © 1993 by Lillenas Publishing Co. All rights reserved.
Administered by Integrated Copyright Group, Inc., P.O. Box 24149, Nashville, TN 37202.

15

18

*"Brethren, We Have Met to Worship" (Atkins - Moore)

*Arr. © 1993 by Lillenas Publishing Co. All rights reserved.
 Administered by Integrated Copyright Group, Inc., P.O. Box 24149, Nashville, TN 37202.

20

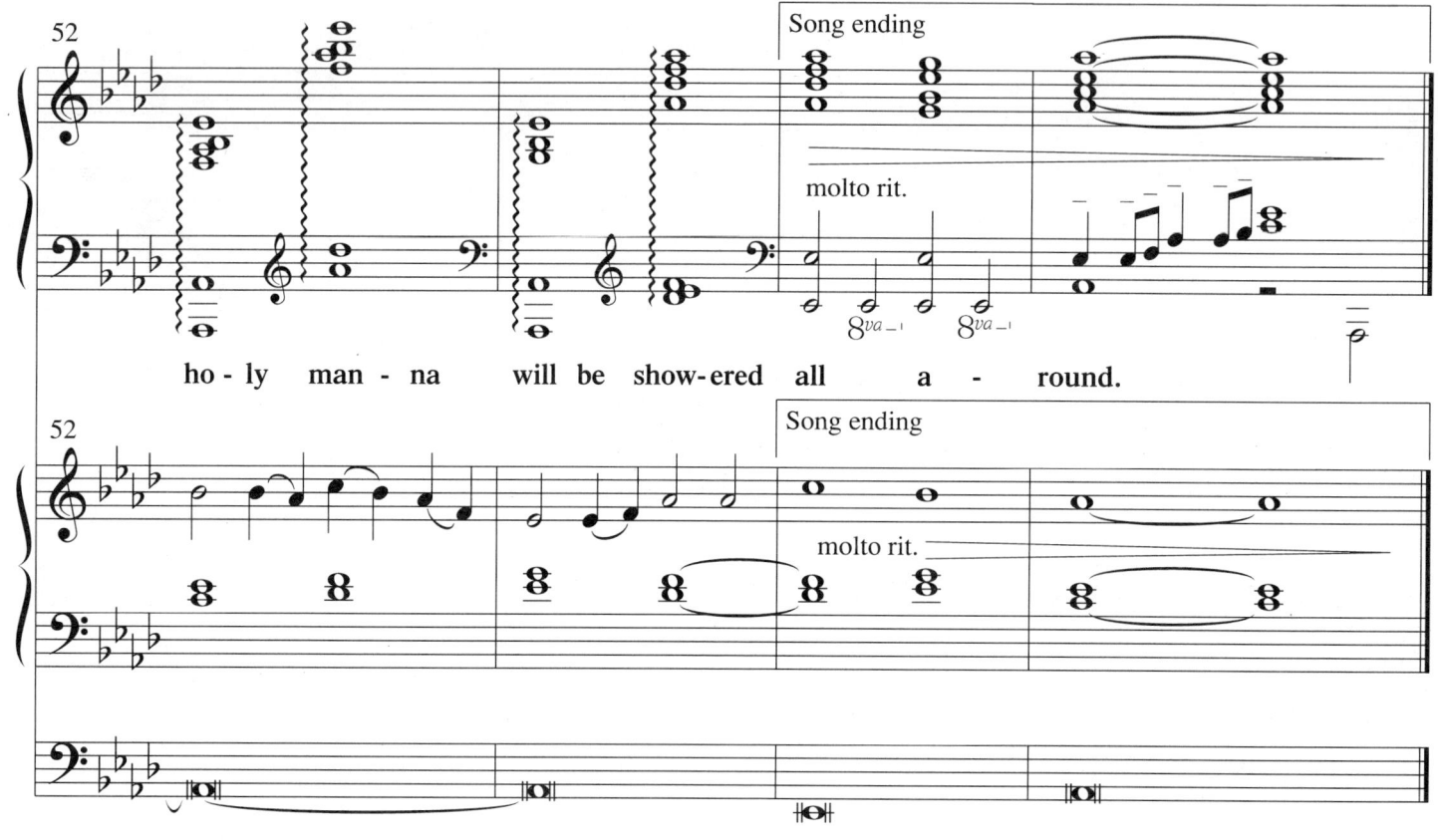

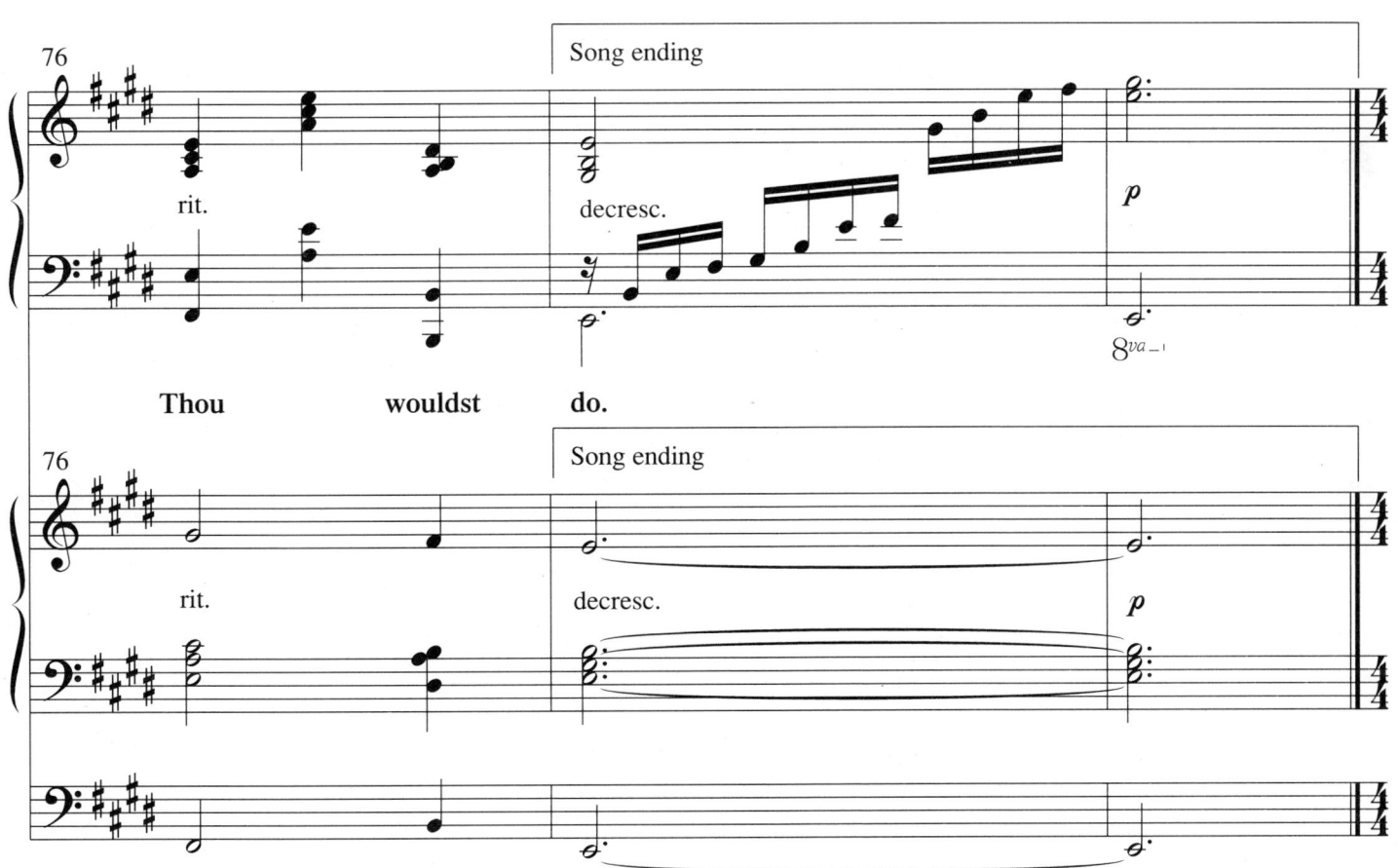

24

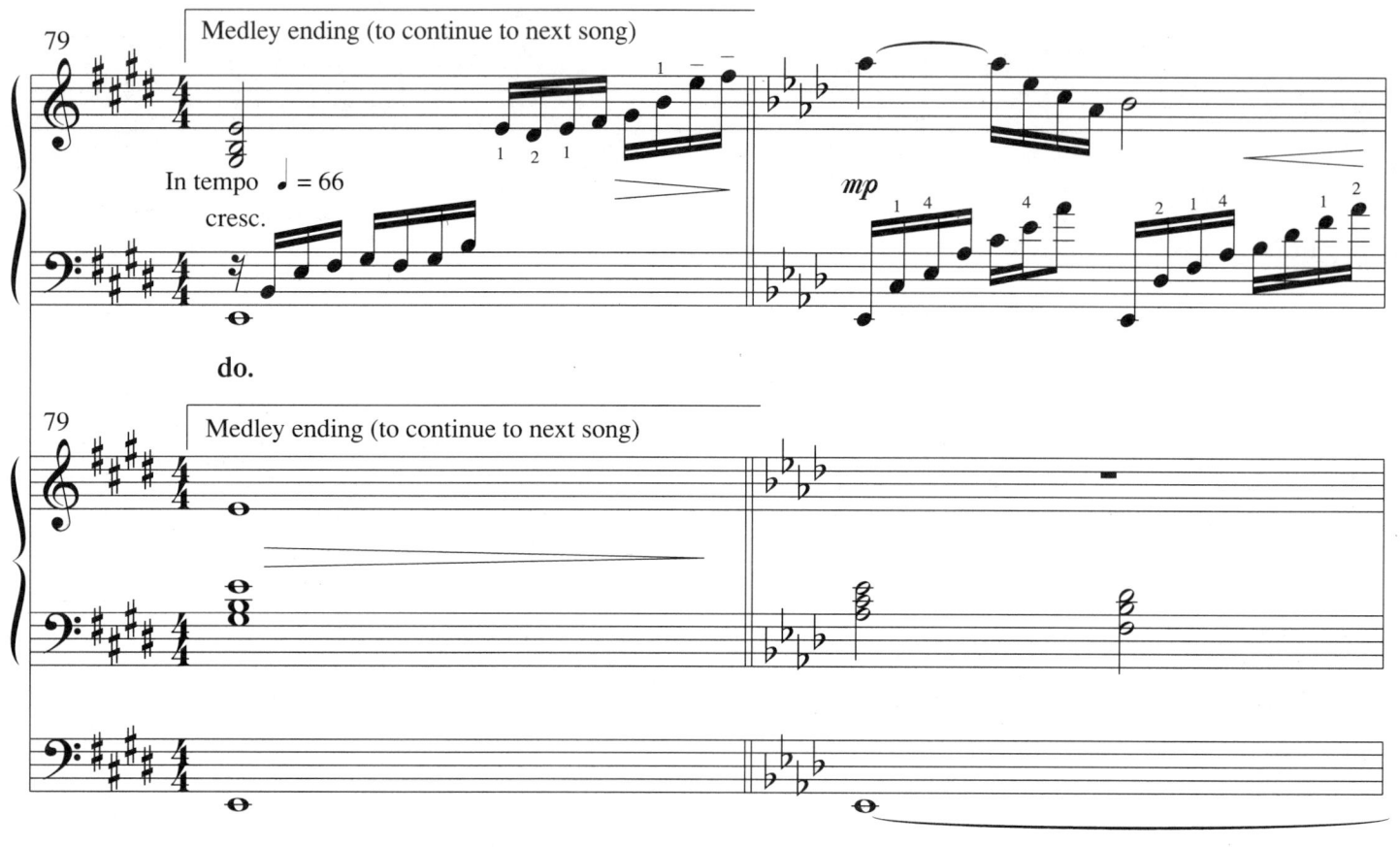

*"Set My Spirit Free" (Anon.)

*Arr. © 1993 by Lillenas Publishing Co. All rights reserved.
Administered by Integrated Copyright Group, Inc., P.O. Box 24149, Nashville, TN 37202.

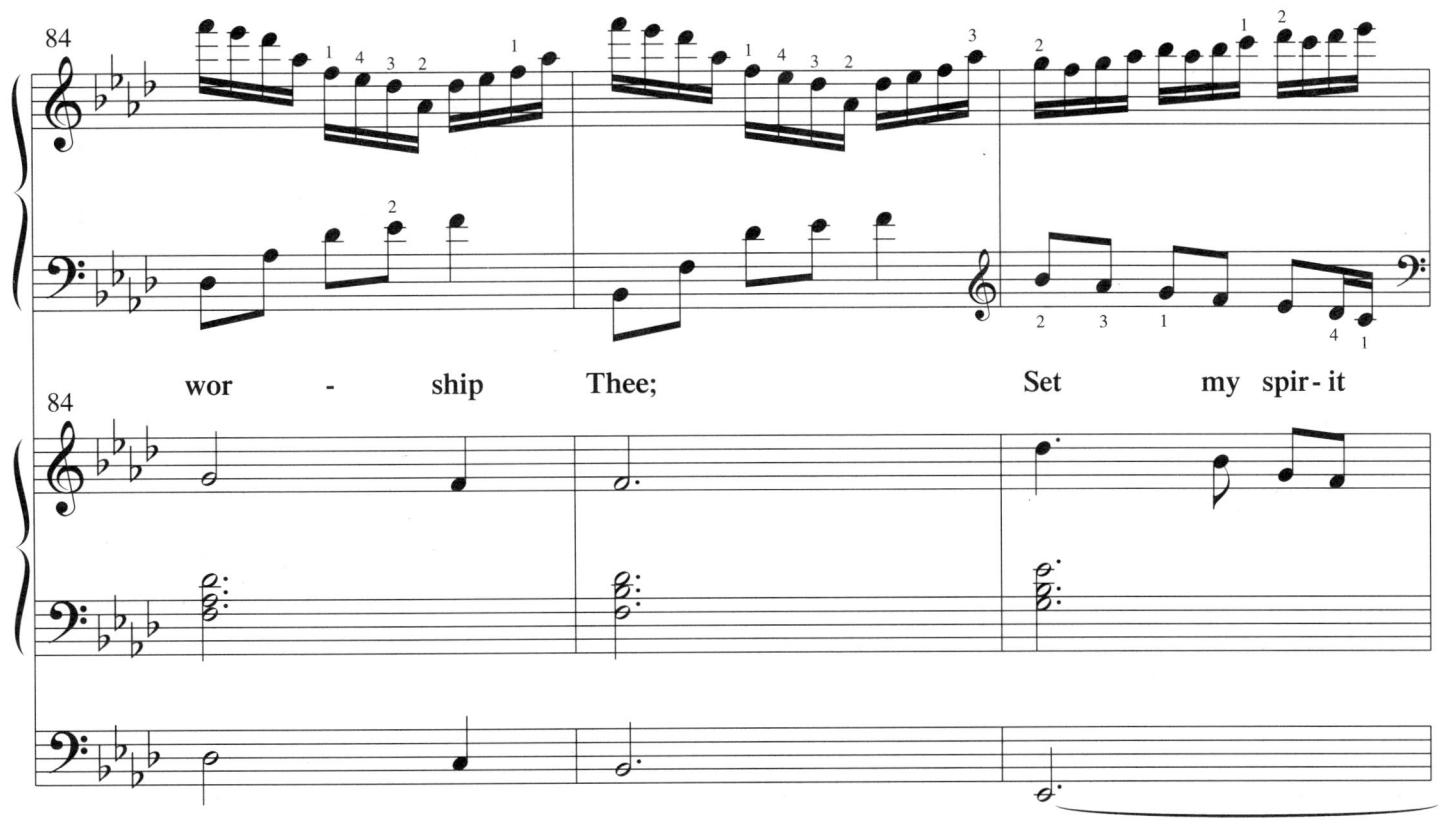

26

27

*"Holy God, We Praise Thy Name"
(Franz, tr. Walworth - *Katholisches Gesangbuch*)

*Arr. © 1993 by Lillenas Publishing Co. All rights reserved.
  Administered by Integrated Copyright Group, Inc., P.O. Box 24149, Nashville, TN 37202.

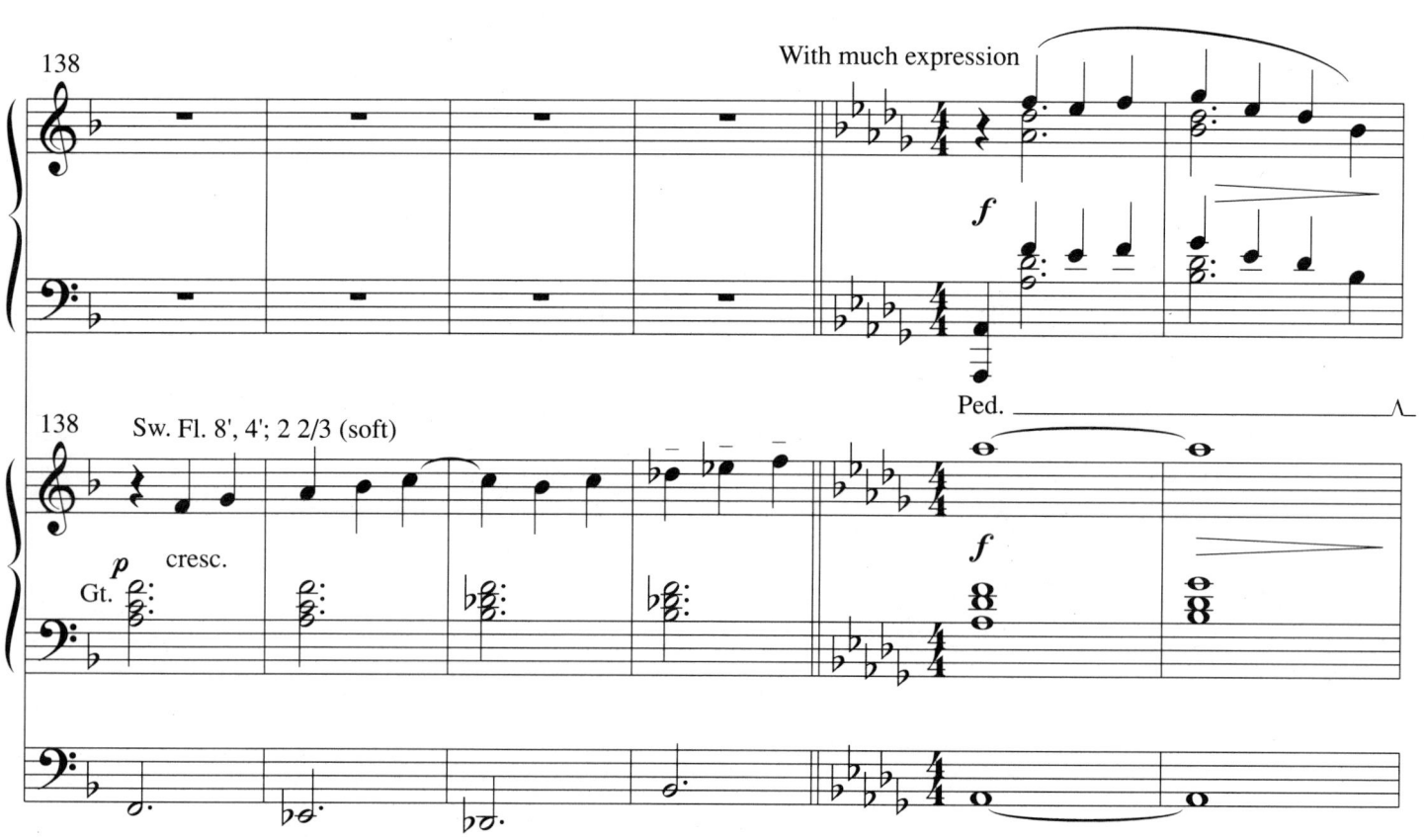

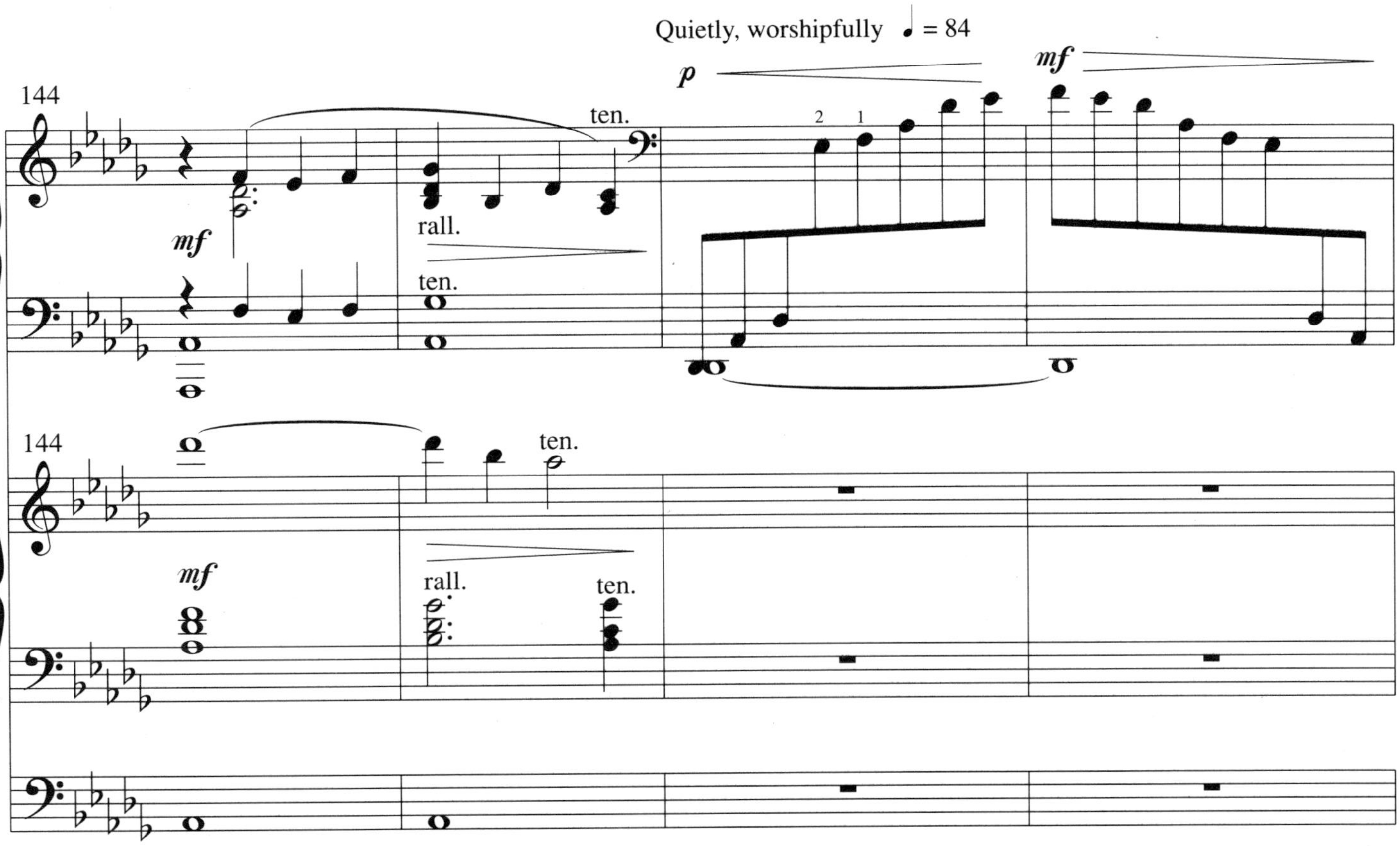

*"I Adore You" (Linda Sprunger) Vocal leadsheet on p. 66

*© 1993 by Lillenas Publishing Co. All rights reserved.
Administered by Integrated Copyright Group, Inc., P.O. Box 24149, Nashville, TN 37202.

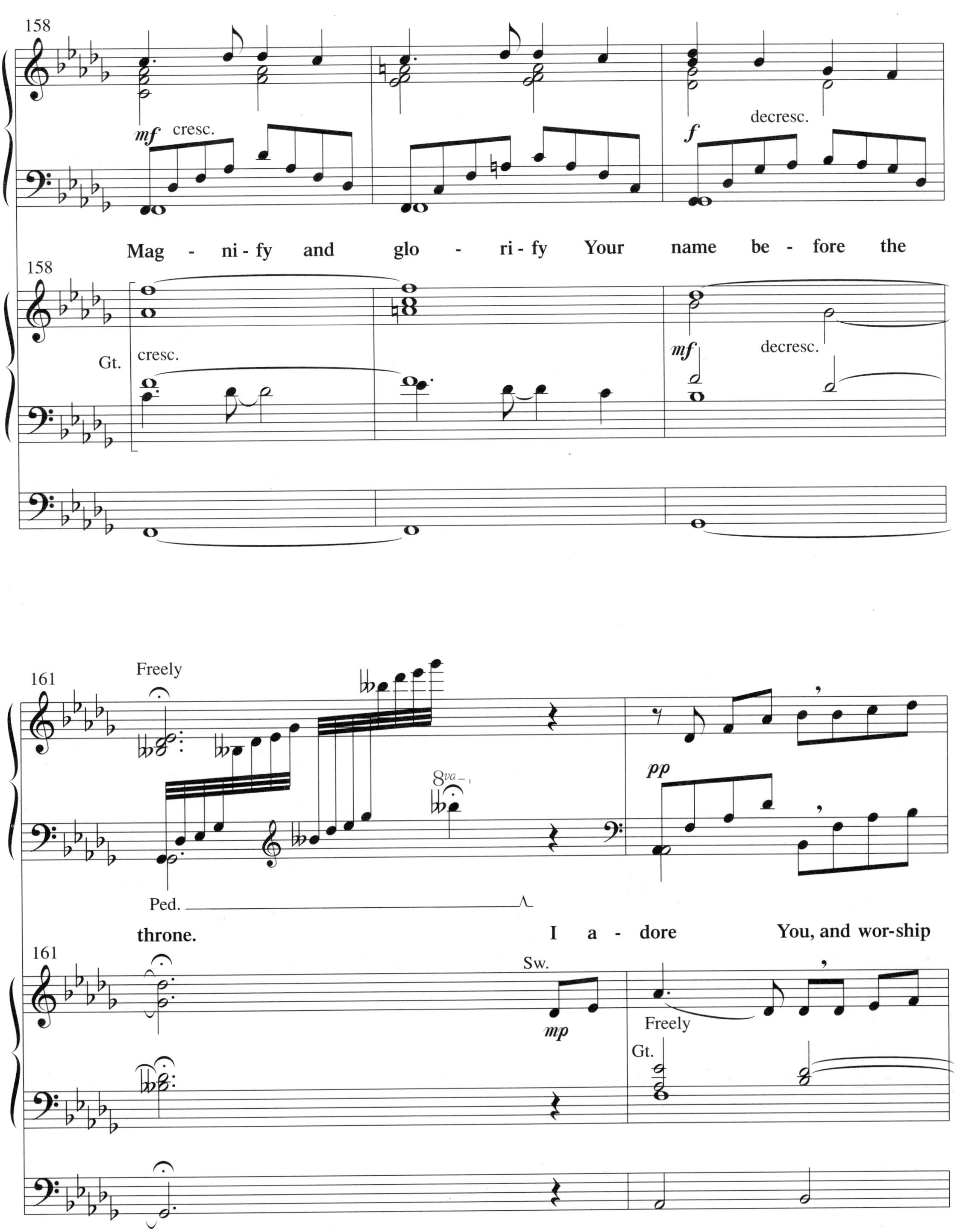
158
mf cresc.
f
decresc.
Mag - ni - fy and glo - ri - fy Your name be - fore the
158
Gt.
cresc.
mf
decresc.
161
Freely
8va
Ped.
pp
throne.
I a - dore You, and wor-ship
161
Sw.
mp
Freely
Gt.

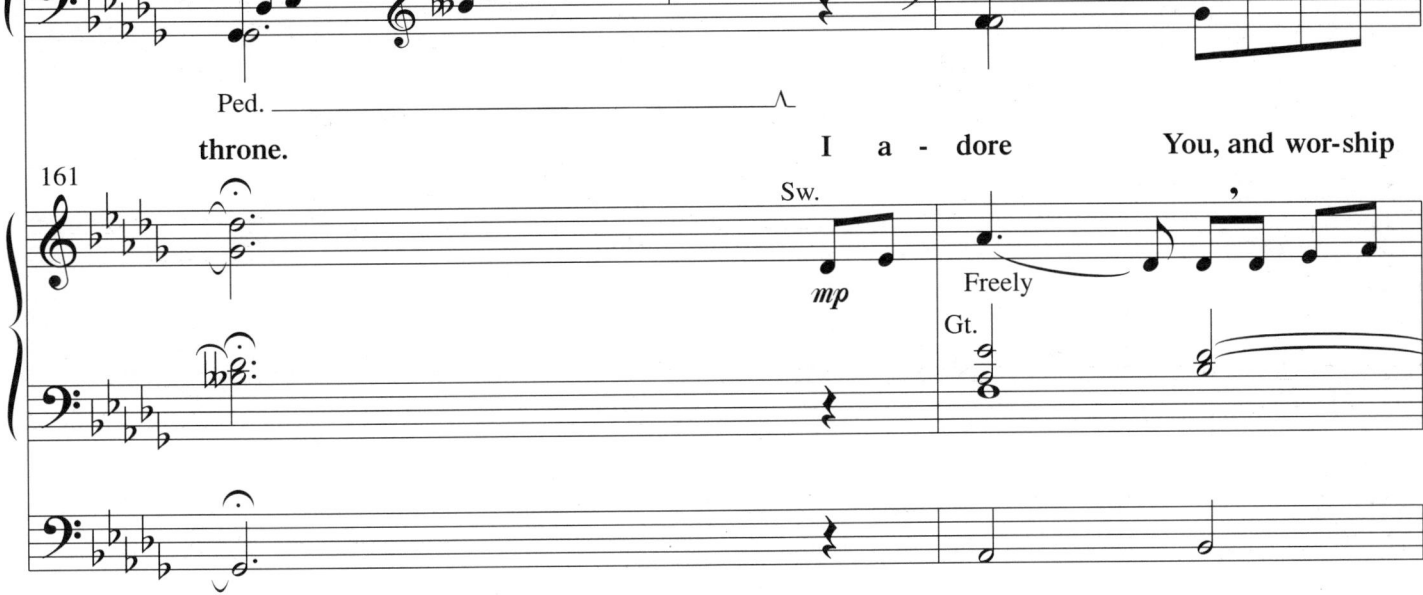

37

*"Fairest Lord Jesus" (Anon., tr. Seiss - *Schlesische Volkslieder*)

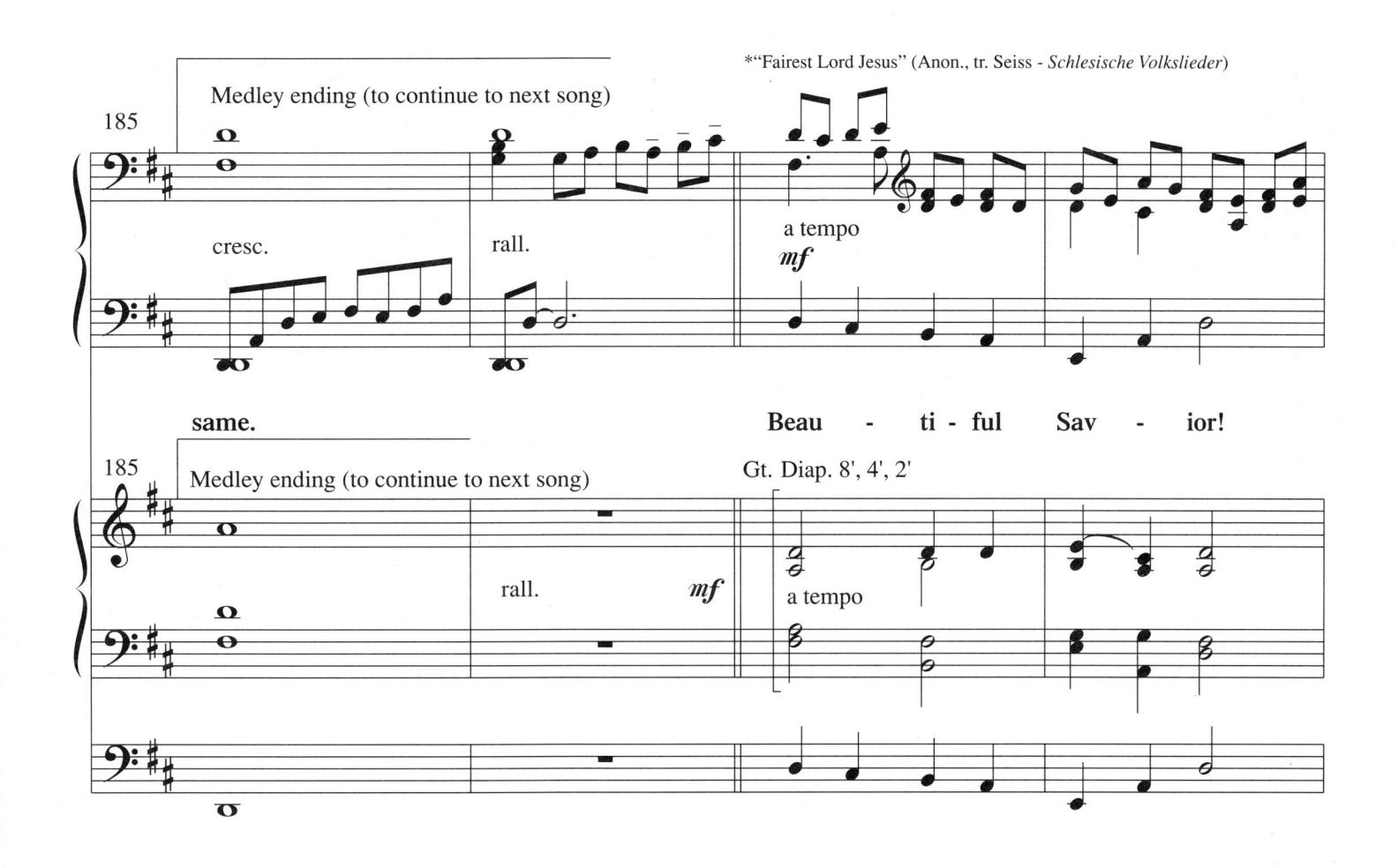

*Arr. © 1993 by Lillenas Publishing Co. All rights reserved.
Administered by Integrated Copyright Group, Inc., P.O. Box 24149, Nashville, TN 37202.

God and Son of Man!

Glo - ry and hon - or, praise, ad - o -

ra - tion, Now and for - ev - er - more be Thine!

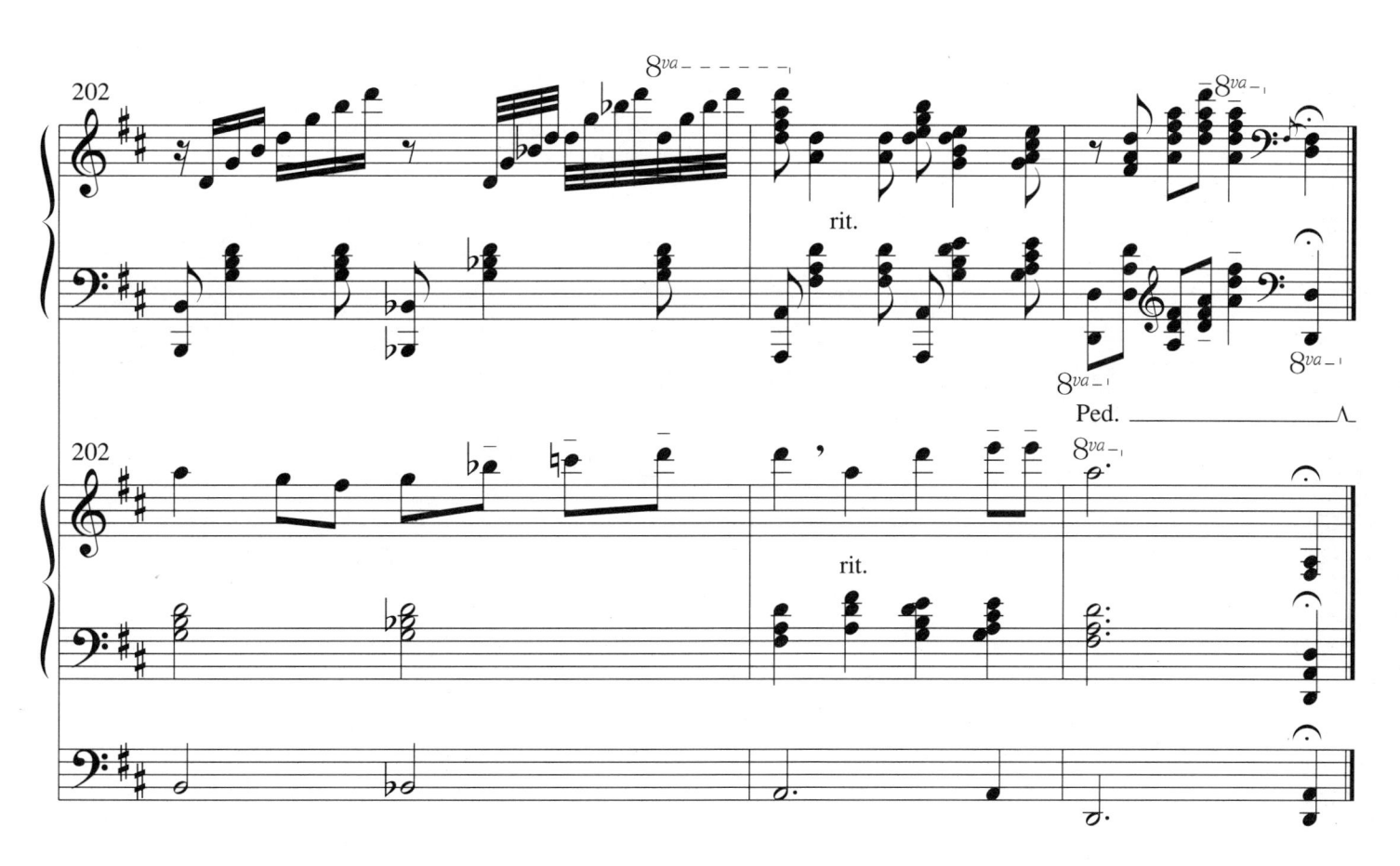

# *Arioso

Sw. Solo Fl. 8', 4', 2 2/3'
Gt. Soft Fl. 8', 4'
Ped. 16', 8'

J. S. BACH
*Arr. by Ron and Linda Sprunger*

---

*See performance notes on pp. 2-3 and optional instrumental solo part on p. 67.

**The use of finger substitution in the organ left-hand part should be practiced thoroughly to obtain a quiet, legato touch throughout. If a solo C-instrument is used, divide the organ left-hand part between both hands.

Arr. © 1993 by Lillenas Publishing Co. All rights reserved.
Administered by Integrated Copyright Group, Inc., P.O. Box 24149, Nashville, TN 37202.

41

42

43

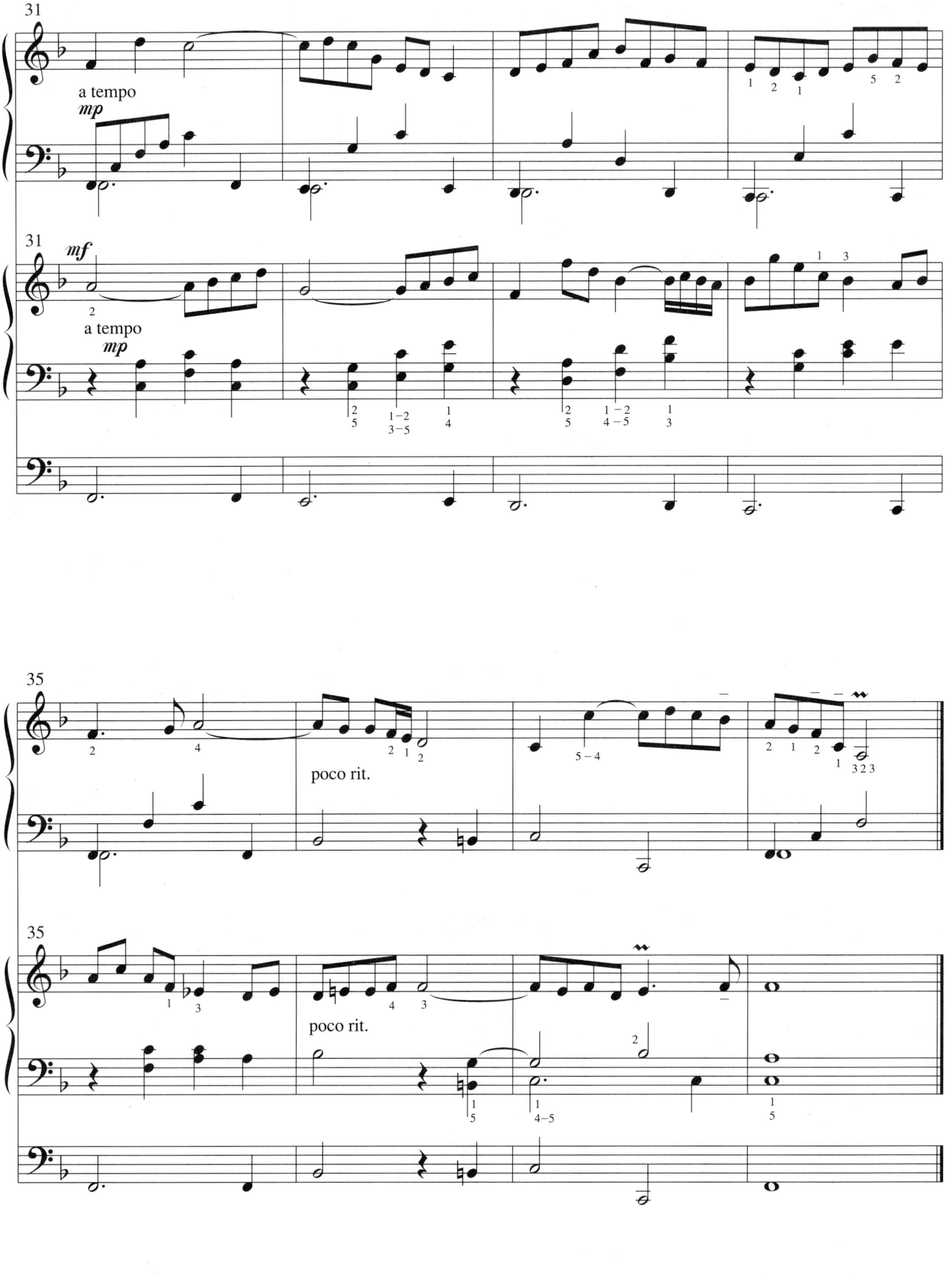
31
a tempo
mp
31
mf
a tempo
mp
35
poco rit.
35
poco rit.

# O Holy Night

Sw. Fl. 8', 4', 2 2/3'
Gt. Soft flutes or strings
Ped. Soft 16', 8'

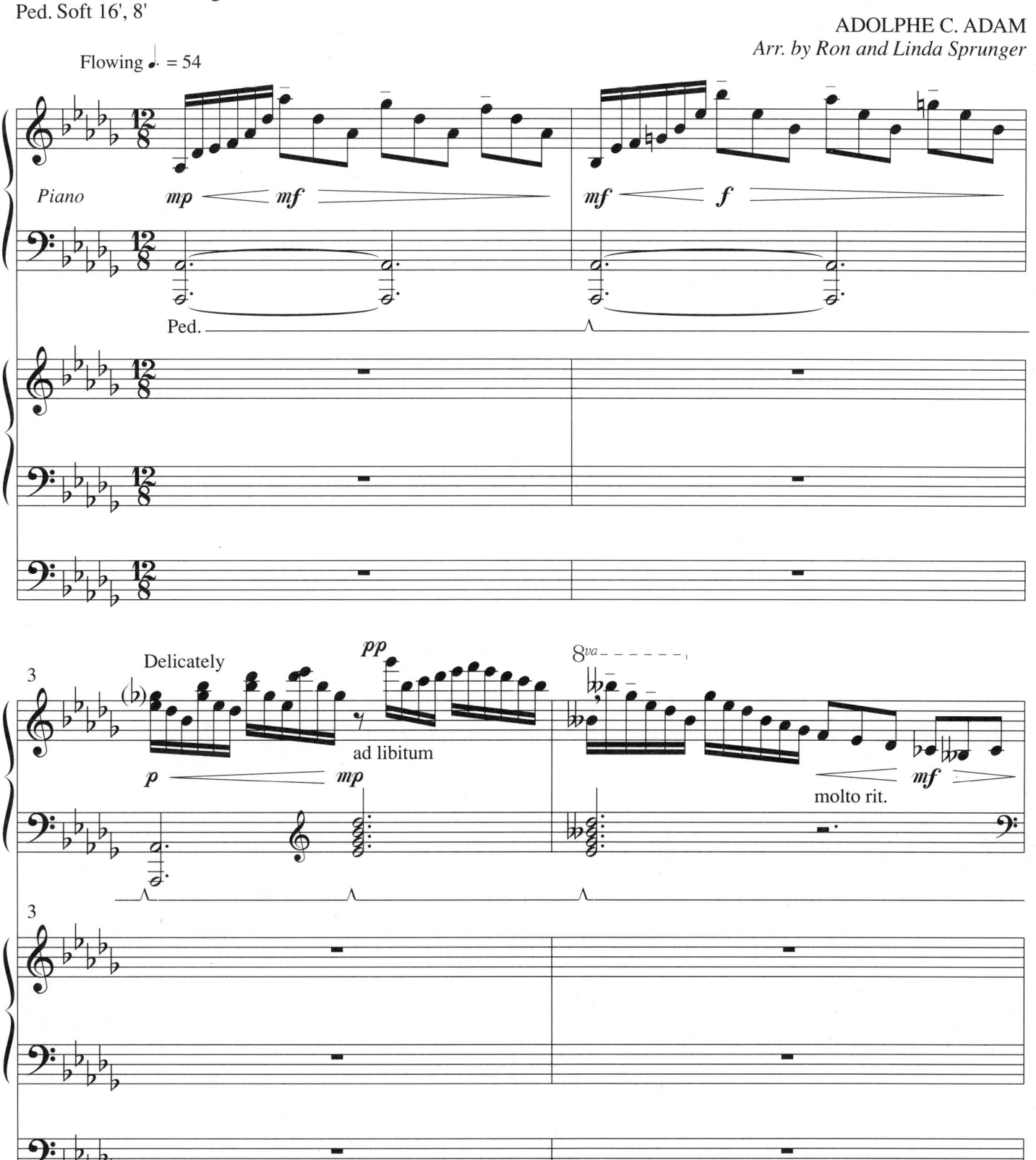

ADOLPHE C. ADAM
*Arr. by Ron and Linda Sprunger*

Arr. © 1993 by Lillenas Publishing Co. All rights reserved.
Administered by Integrated Copyright Group, Inc., P.O. Box 24149, Nashville, TN 37202.

46

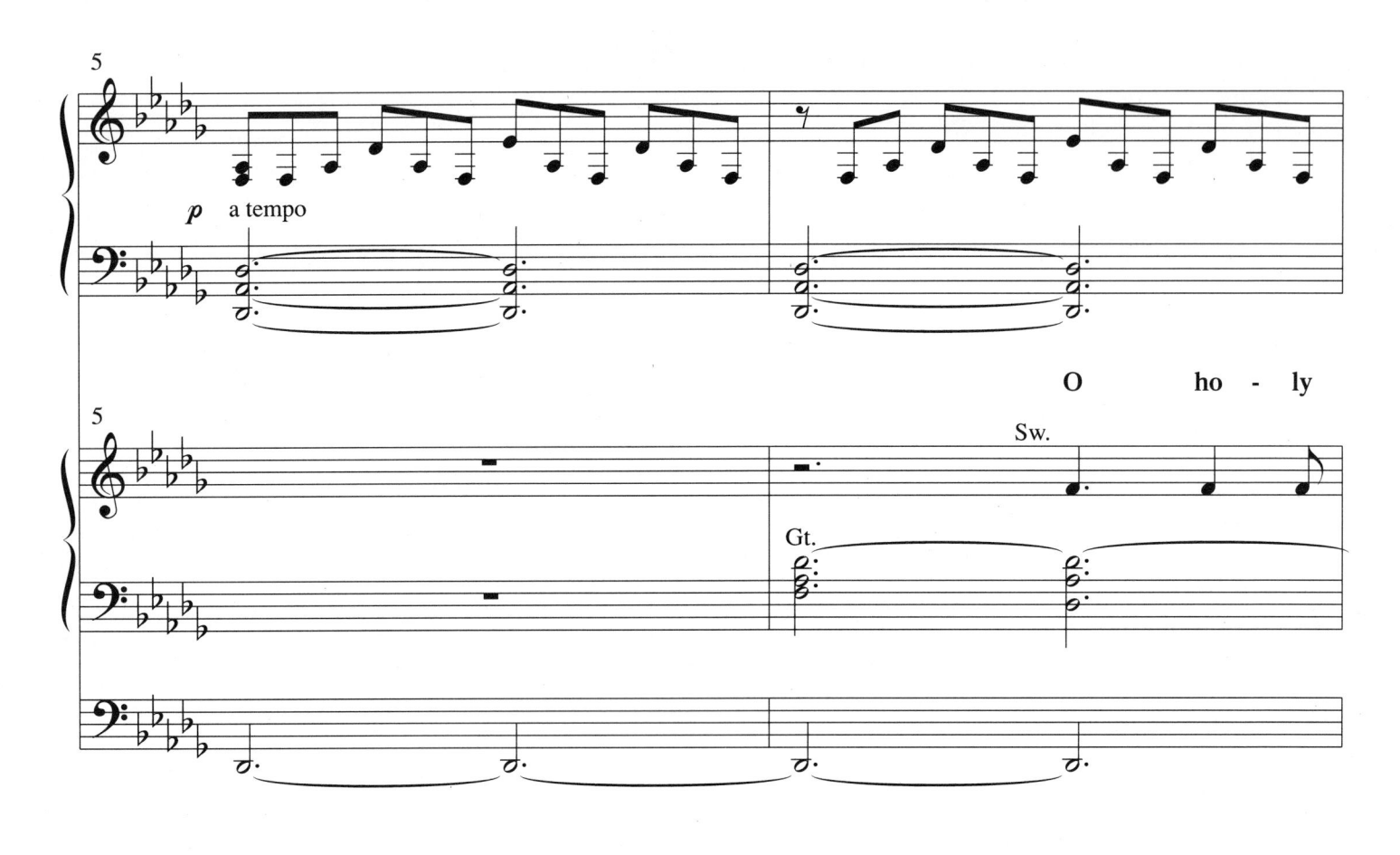

night of the dear Sav - ior's birth.

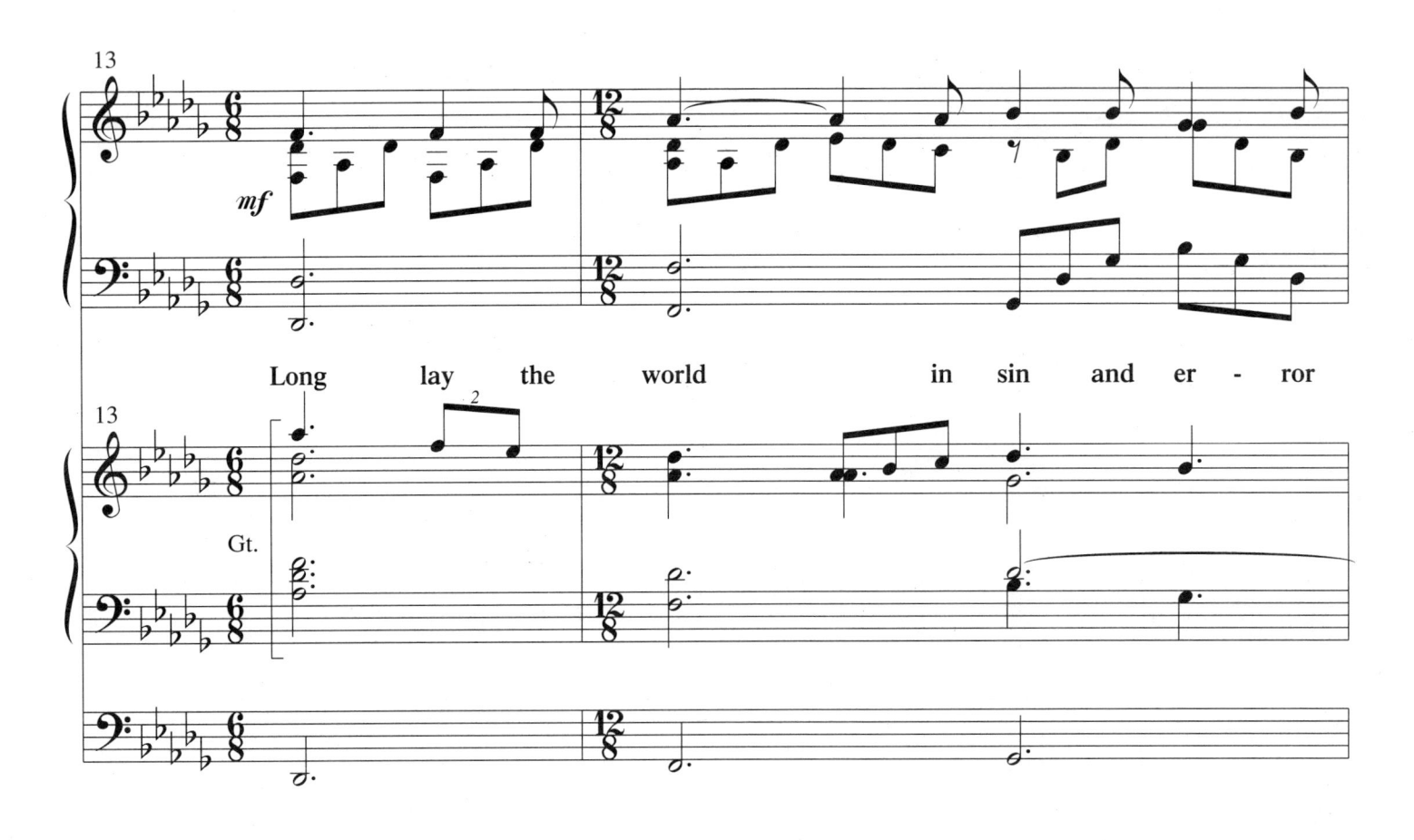

Long lay the world in sin and er - ror pin - ing, Till He ap - peared and the soul felt its worth. A thrill of hope— the weary world rejoices, For yonder breaks a

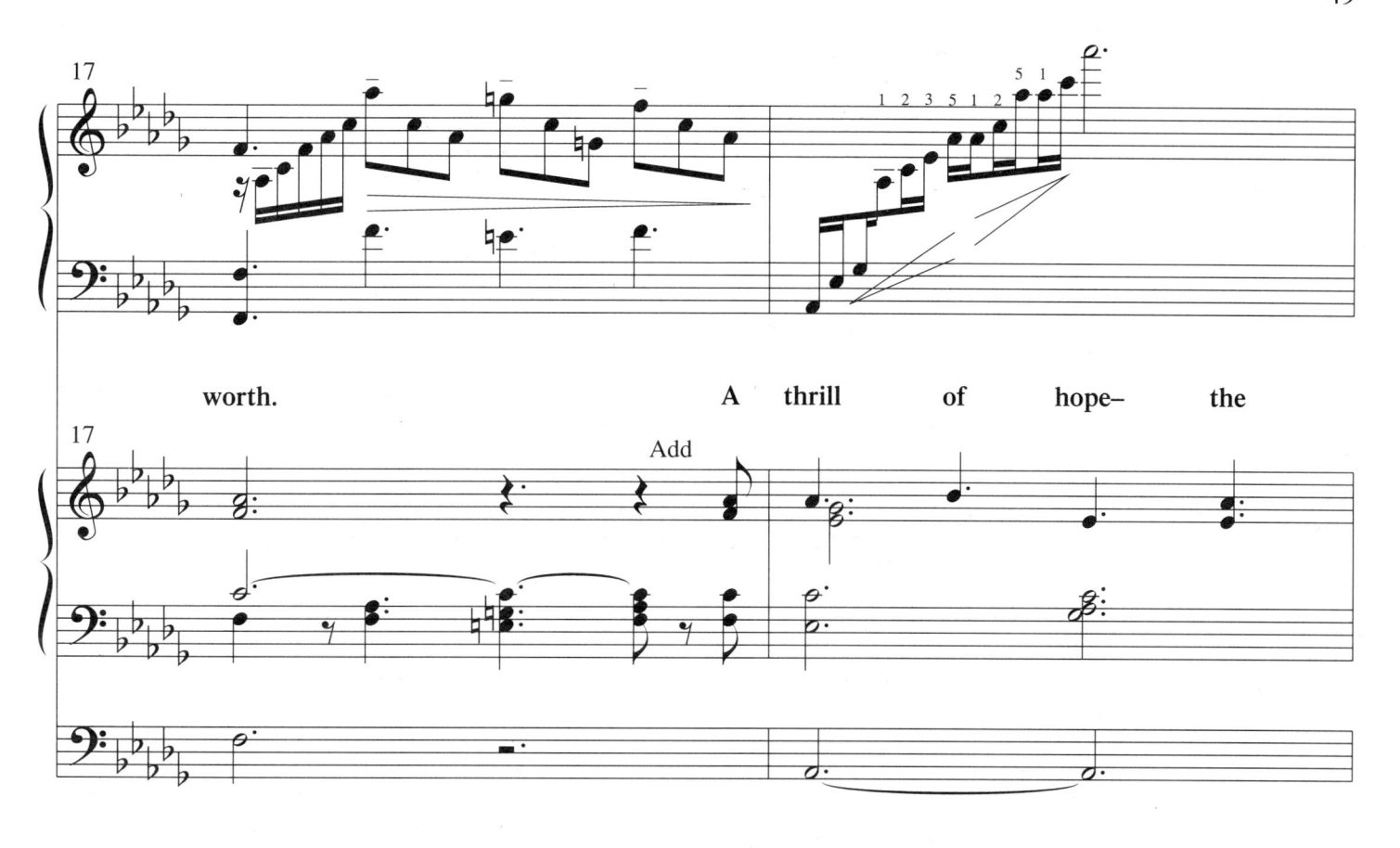

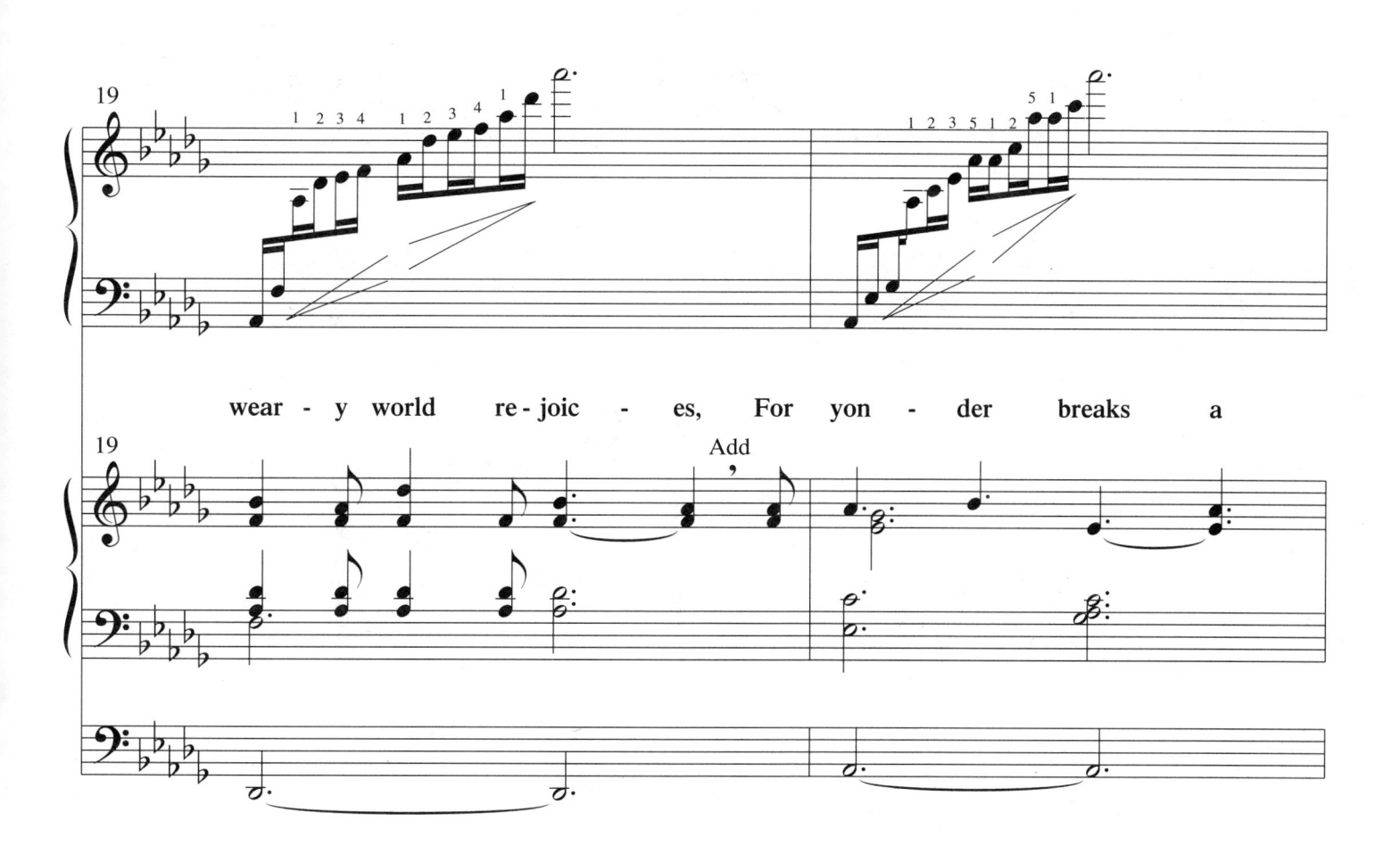

new and glo-rious morn! Fall on your
Christ is the

knees! O hear the an-gel
Lord! O praise His name for-

51

born! ... O night di-
claim! His
vine! O night, O night di-
Reduce

vine! pow'r and glo-ry ev-er-more pro-claim!

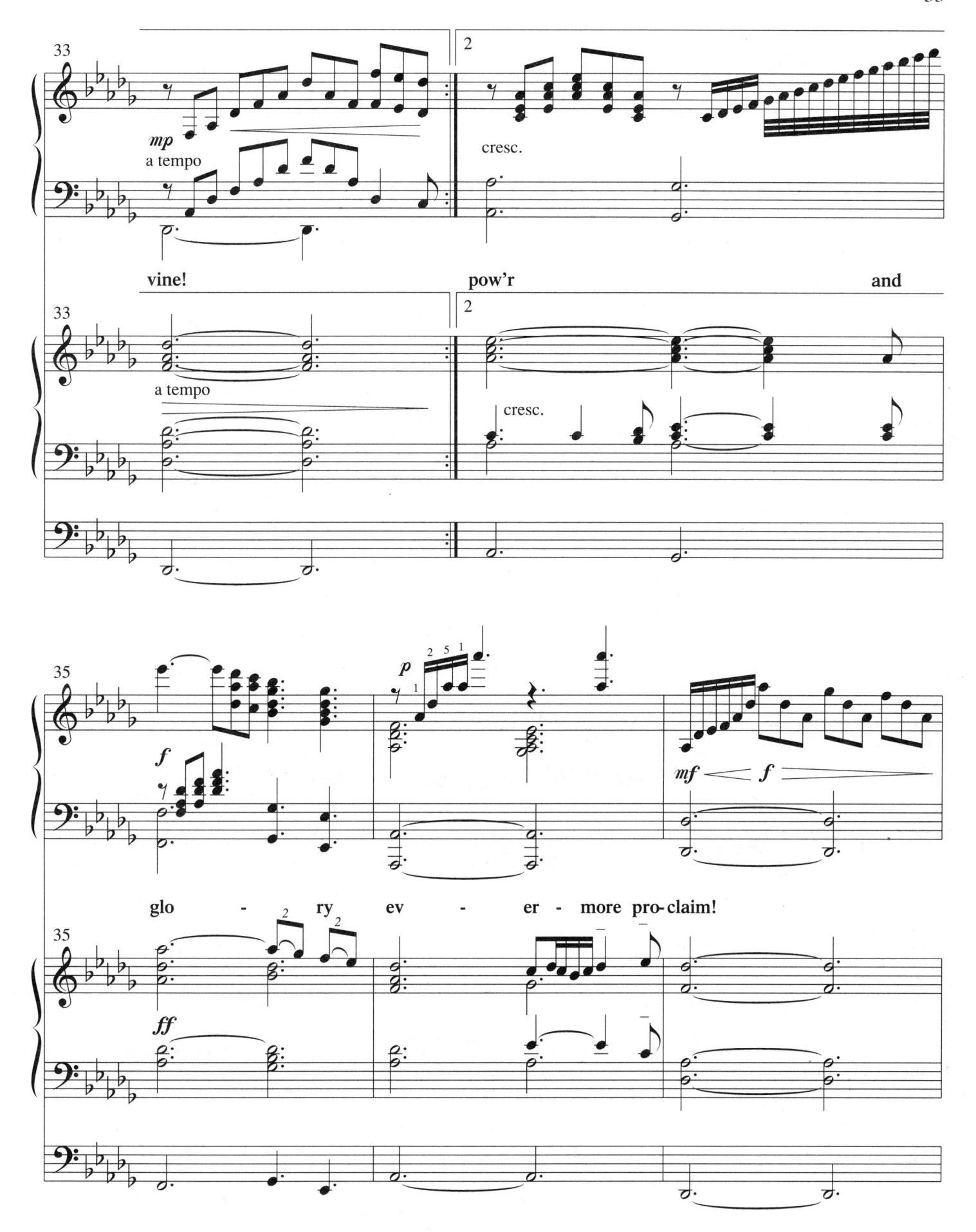

38
mp
mf
p
mp
38
Sw. soft solo stop
p
Gt.
mp
8va
40
Lightly, freely
decresc.
8
8
8
8va
Ped.
40
decresc.

# Near the Cross of Jesus
## (Medley)

Sw. Solo Fl. (or soft reed)
Gt. Celeste
Ped. Soft 16', 8'

*Arr. by Ron and Linda Sprunger*

Flowing, expressive

*"Near the Cross" (Crosby – Doane)

Je-sus, keep me near the cross. There a pre-cious foun-tain, Free to all, a

*Arr. © 1993 by Lillenas Publishing Co. All rights reserved.
Administered by Integrated Copyright Group, Inc., P.O. Box 24149, Nashville, TN 37202.

11
rall.
a tempo
heal - ing stream,
Flows from Cal - v'ry's
11
rall.
a tempo
15
mf
moun - tain.
In the cross, in the
15
Sw.
f
mf
Gt.

cross Be my glo - ry ev - er, Till my rap - tured soul shall find Rest be - yond the riv - er.

33
Delicately
pp
poco rall.
a tempo
simile
Near the cross, a trem - bling soul, Love and
33
Sw. Solo Fl. (or soft reed)
mp
Gt.
p
poco rall.
a tempo
38
mer - cy found me; There the Bright and
38

Morn - ing Star Sheds its beams a - round me.

*Delicately*

In the cross, in the cross Be my glo - ry ev - er,

Gt. Celeste

*pp*

rit.

Till my rap-tured soul shall find

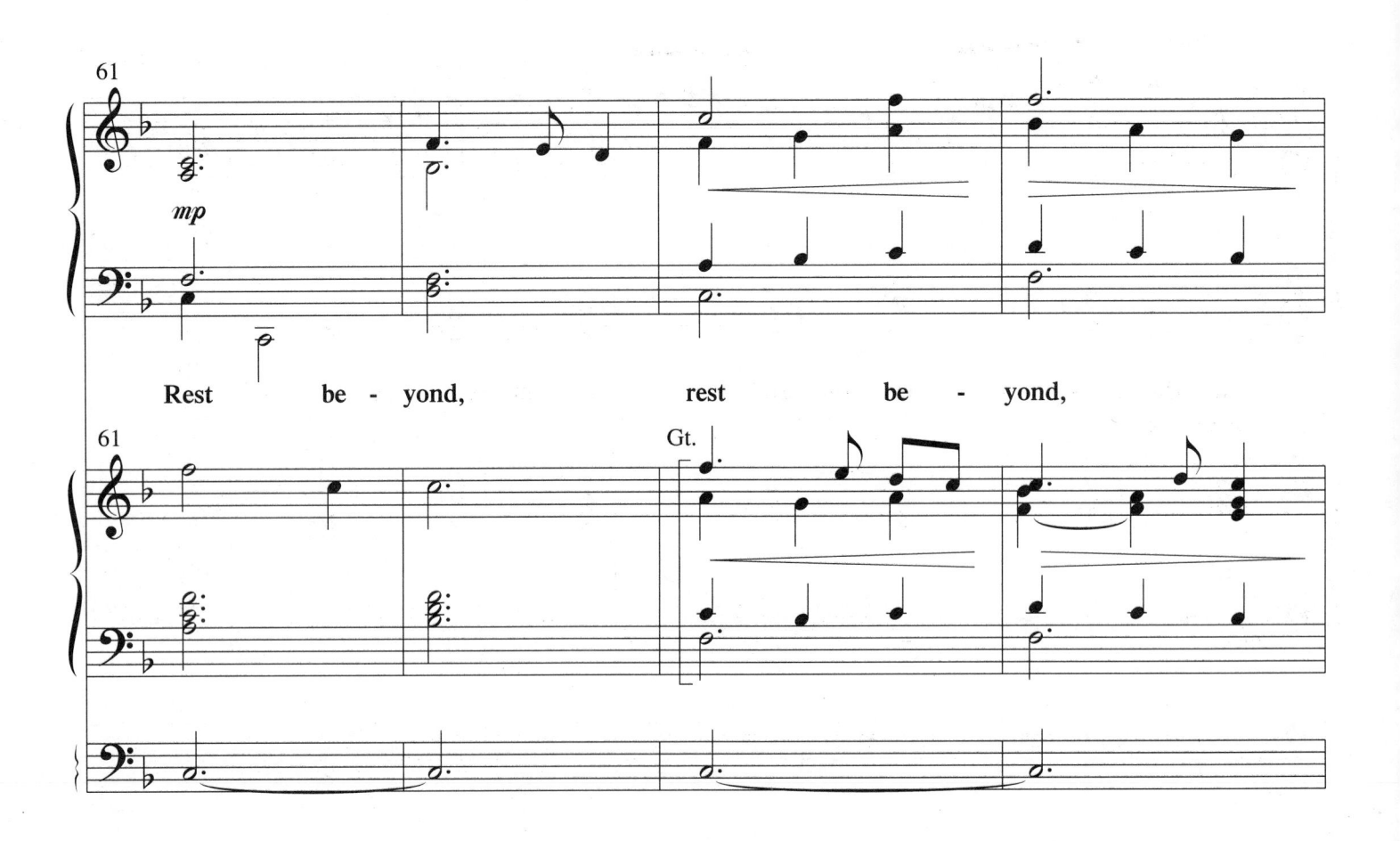

Rest be-yond, rest be-yond,

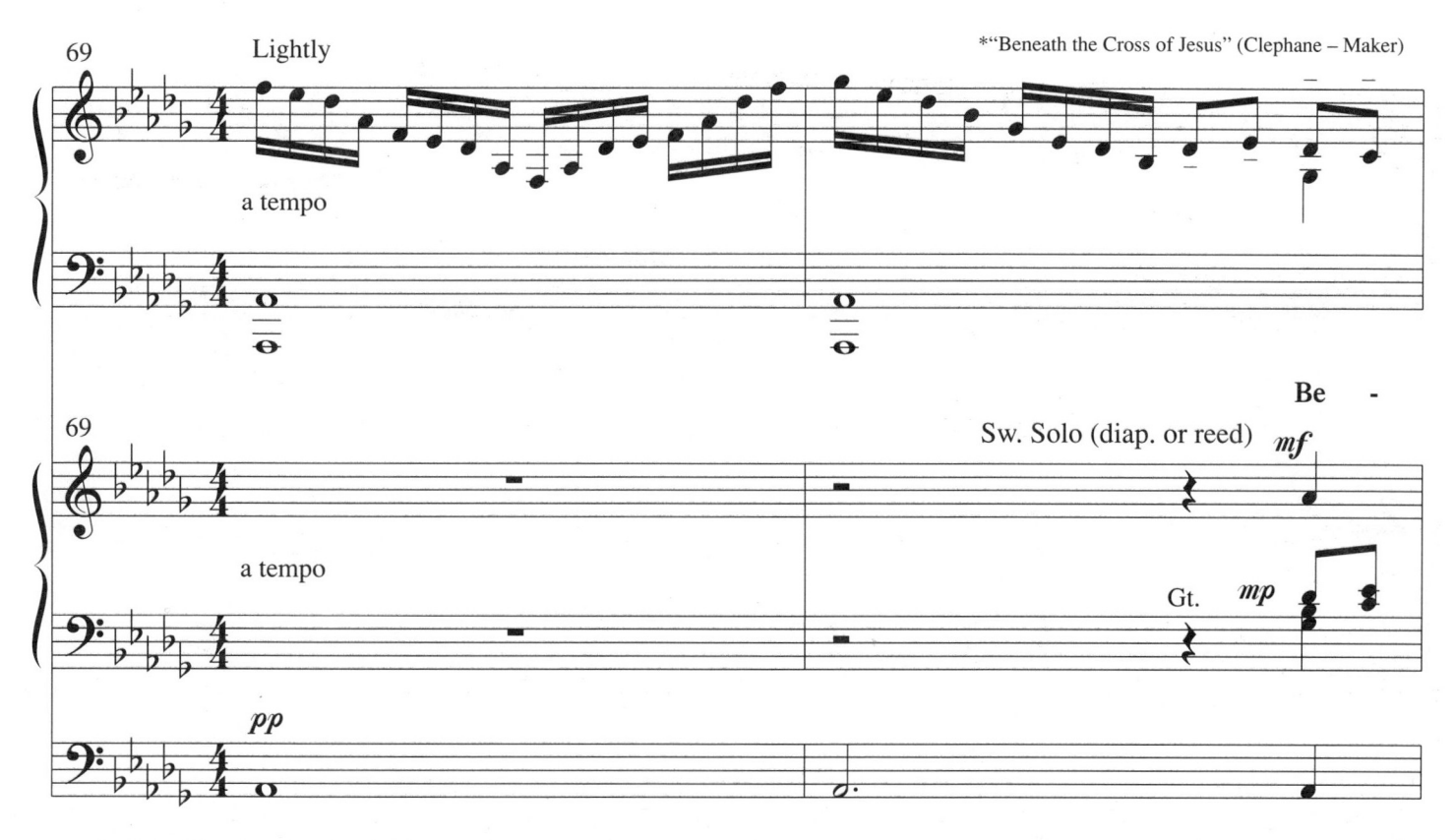

rest be - yond the riv - er.

Lightly

*"Beneath the Cross of Jesus" (Clephane – Maker)

a tempo

Sw. Solo (diap. or reed) *mf*

Be -

Gt. *mp*

*Arr. © 1993 by Lillenas Publishing Co. All rights reserved.
Administered by Integrated Copyright Group, Inc., P.O. Box 24149, Nashville, TN 37202.

71
Ped.
sim.
neath the cross of Je - sus I
71
73
fain would take my stand–
The
73

sha - dow of a might - y rock With -
in a wea - ry land, A

home with-in the wil - der - ness, A rest up-on the way From the burn - ing of the noon - tide heat   And the bur - den of the   day.

# I Adore You

L. S.

LINDA SPRUNGER

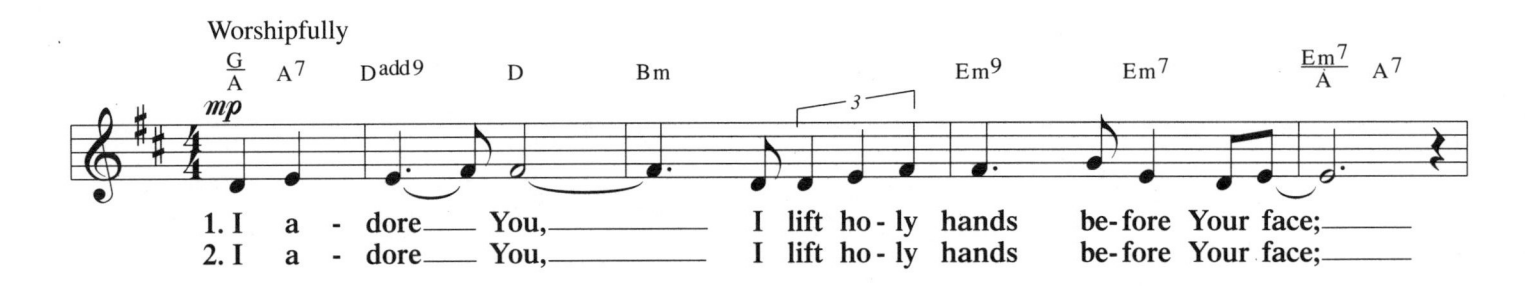

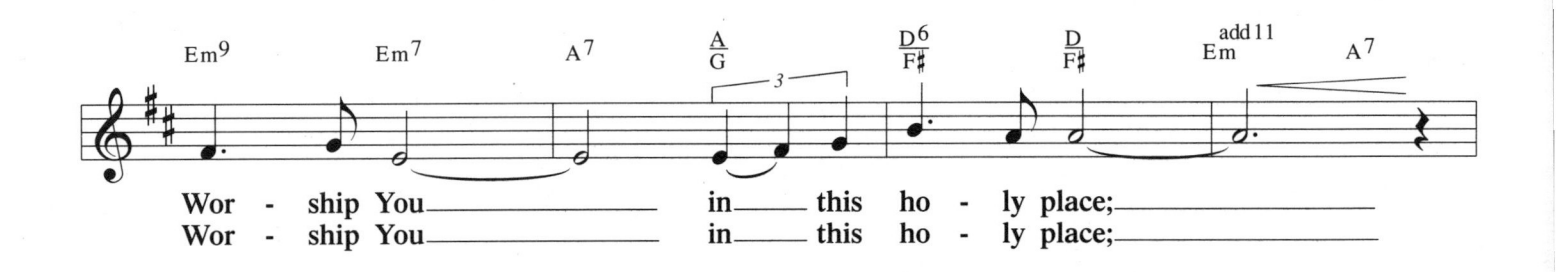

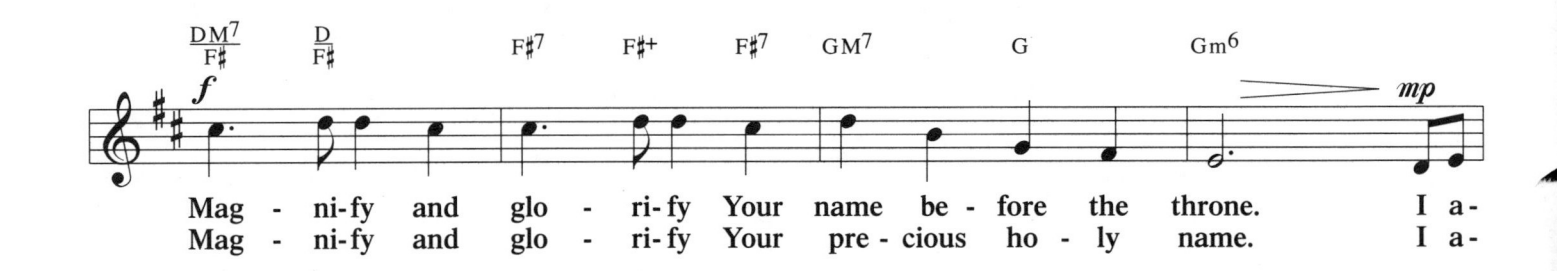

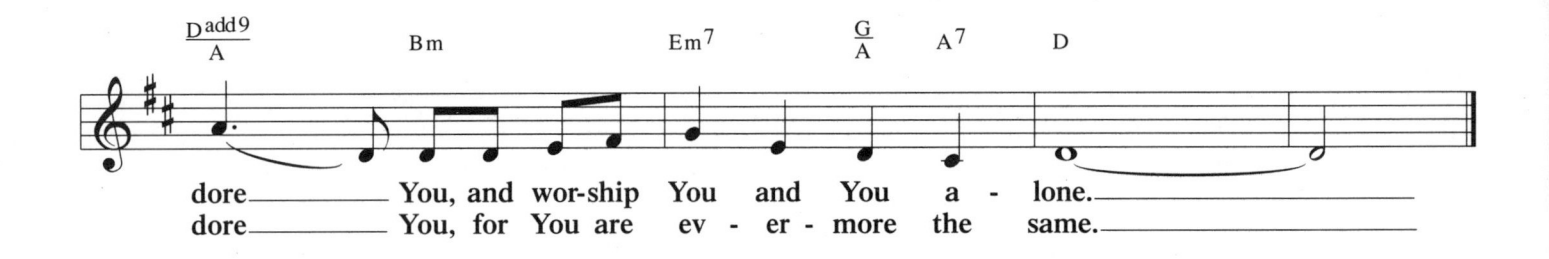

Worshipfully

1. I a-dore You, I lift ho-ly hands be-fore Your face;
2. I a-dore You, I lift ho-ly hands be-fore Your face;

Wor-ship You in this ho-ly place;
Wor-ship You in this ho-ly place;

Mag-ni-fy and glo-ri-fy Your name be-fore the throne. I a-
Mag-ni-fy and glo-ri-fy Your pre-cious ho-ly name. I a-

dore You, and wor-ship You and You a-lone.
dore You, for You are ev-er-more the same.

© 1993 by Lillenas Publishing Co. All rights reserved.
Administered by Integrated Copyright Group, Inc., P.O. Box 24149, Nashville, TN 37202.

# Arioso

(C Instrument solo)

J. S. BACH
*Arr. by Ron and Linda Sprunger*